Salad Savvy

Go for the Green

Just like anything else you prepare, choose the freshest, highest-quality ingredients you can find when making salads. It makes the difference between a mediocre salad and a show-stopper.

Shopping

Greens

- Wh... col...

- If p... freshness date and use on or before that date.

- Wash packaged greens even when they are advertised as being pre-washed.

Other Produce

- Color and sheen are not always good indicators of freshness. Some companies dye and wax their produce to make them look more vibrant. Instead, look to make sure there aren't any damaged spots, bruises, mold or withering.

- Fruit should be fragrant, without any "off" odors. For example, pre-bagged citrus fruits can hide moldy fruit that cannot be detected by the eye but can certainly be sought out by the nose.

- When shopping for produce, pick it up. Make sure it feels heavy for its size. Fruits and vegetables typically lose moisture through the skin with age.

Wash on Gentle; Spin Dry

Water is needed to wash your salad greens but is also the archenemy against a good salad, as it dilutes dressings and makes for slimy greens. Enter the **Salad and Berry Spinner** to save the day.

How does a salad spinner work?

Physics! The spinning action creates centrifugal force to draw the moisture toward the outside of the colander.

When preparing greens, pick through them and remove any shriveled, discolored or bruised leaves. If the greens are slightly wilted, you can soak them in ice-cold water for a few minutes to perk them up.

To wash greens, place them into the large colander of the spinner and rinse them under cold running water until clean. You can wash and dry fresh herbs in the spinner, too. Depending on the amount of herbs you're using, you can use the small or large colander.

Help the spinner do its job; don't overpack it. Also, shake excess water from the colander before spinning the greens dry.

It will probably take several spins to thoroughly dry greens. Spin them a few times, then drain the water out of the bowl. Repeat until the bowl is dry after spinning.

To wash spinach, fill the spinner bowl with cold water. Fill the colander with spinach, dunk it in the water, and swish to release dirt. Lift the colander out of the water and repeat until the water runs clear. Spin dry.

All That Other Good Stuff

Let your creativity run wild with different ingredients and flavors. Here are some tips for success:

Be Careful of Too Much Moisture
- *The seeds in vegetables such as cucumbers and tomatoes contain a lot of moisture, making salads soggy. Remove the seeds before serving them.*

- *It's best to keep heavier ingredients such as tomato wedges separated from the greens until it's serving time. Otherwise, they will crush the greens and make them soggy.*

Less is More
- *It may be tempting, but don't pack too many different flavors into one salad. Save some of it for another creation on another day.*

Dress It up

Always dress green salads at the last minute for best flavor, texture and appearance. And don't drown salad with dressing. A light coating of dressing brings out the flavor in the greens and other ingredients.

Vinaigrettes

There's a bit of physical science involved to make a vinaigrette work. But all you need to know is that the basic vinaigrette ratio is typically two parts oil to one part acid seasoned with salt and black pepper. The rest is up to you.

Vinaigrettes, considered temporary emulsions because the oil and vinegar separate with time, can be mastered with a few key tricks:

When making a vinaigrette, it is important to add the oil in a slow, steady stream, whisking continuously. Some chefs even recommend going drop-by-drop!

Oil used to make vinaigrette should be at room temperature or the emulsion will be harder to create.

Never fear: you can always re-whisk vinaigrettes if they separate.

Creamy Dressings

Examples of permanent emulsions include creamy salad dressings and mayonnaise.

More on Vinaigrettes

- *To let all of the flavors in your salad dressing shine, hydrate dried herbs and spices in the acid...then slowly whisk in the oil. If you whisk in the oil before the dried ingredients have a chance to hydrate, they get bound up in the oil, leaving you with dried bits with a harsh, bitter bite.*

- *To make your vinaigrette stay blended longer, whisk in a little mustard, yogurt or buttermilk.*

You can tailor a vinaigrette with a few tweaks to the basic formula. Here are just a few examples to get you started:

Oils
- *Olive oil, canola oil, sesame oil, nut oils such as walnut, flavored oils such as our Basil Blend Canola Oil or Garlic-Infused Canola Oil.*

Acids/Vinegars
- *White or red wine vinegar, white or regular balsamic vinegar, flavored vinegars, rice vinegar, apple cider vinegar, even champagne vinegar, any type of citrus juice, from lemon juice to key lime to blood orange, fruit juices that are reduced to a syrup.*

Flavoring Ingredients
- *Aromatics like garlic, shallots or onions; herbs; spices; sugar in any form; specialty mustards; wasabi paste; red curry paste; salsa; barbecue sauce.*

The Skinny on Salads

Here's the golden rule: the more **colorful** the salad, the better for you it is. But no cheating. Limit the amount of add-ons that didn't come from a garden, no matter how colorful they may be.

Choose and prepare ingredients wisely for maximum nutritional impact.

In general, darker green leafy vegetables, such as romaine lettuce, spinach and arugula, contain more nutrients than iceberg lettuce.

Fruit is a colorful, flavorful and healthy addition to just about any salad. To complement the season, choose fruit such as apples or pears to go with the cooler months, and mangoes or berries during warmer weather.

To preserve vitamins when preparing fresh vegetables, store them properly and use them soon after purchasing.

Keep the peels on vegetables with dark-colored skins such as zucchini or radishes and fruits such as apples.

If cooking salad ingredients, don't overcook them and if possible, steam, rather than boil them (most vitamins are water soluble, so boiling leeches the nutrients out of the foods).

Healthy Trade-offs

Don't let too many "add-ons" negate the nutritional benefits of your salad! Make a few healthy substitutions instead:

Go Nuts!
- *Toasted nuts or sunflower seeds add an irresistible crunch and have nutritional value that far outweighs croutons.*

Bits of Goodness
- *Dried fruit is a fun way to perk up the flavor and add a chewy texture while providing antioxidants, which is more than anyone can say about salt- and fat-laden deli meats, bacon or cheese.*

In Pursuit of Protein
- *If your salad will be served as the main course, be sure to include protein, but keep it on the lighter side. For example, choose leaner cuts of beef, and avoid breaded or skin-on chicken. Some examples of lean protein include kidney beans or garbanzo beans, boneless, skinless chicken or turkey breast or tuna packed in water.*

Dress Down for the Occasion
- *If you want to drastically cut down on calories and fat, eschew salad dressing altogether. Simply squeeze a lemon or lime wedge over your salad and sprinkle it with a little salt and coarsely ground black pepper.*

Barbecued Chicken & Roasted Corn Salad

Barbecued Chicken & Roasted Corn Salad

Blackening the vegetables takes this barbecued salad to a new level, infusing every bite with a smoky and sweet flavor.

Marinade and Dressing

- 1/4 cup (50 mL) lime juice
- 2 tbsp (30 mL) **Sweet & Smoky Barbecue Rub**
- 2 garlic cloves, pressed
- 1/2 tsp (2 mL) ground cumin
- 1/2 tsp (2 mL) salt
- 1/4 cup (50 mL) vegetable oil

Chicken and Salad

- 4 boneless, skinless chicken breast halves (4-6 oz/125-175 g each)
- *Barbecue Tortilla Chips* (optional, see Chef's Corner)
- 1 tsp (5 mL) vegetable oil
- 2 cups (500 mL) fresh corn kernels
- 1/2 medium red bell pepper, diced
- 1/4 cup (50 mL) diced red onion
- 1/2 cup (125 mL) canned black beans, rinsed and drained
- 2 cups (500 mL) julienne-cut jicama strips

Prep time: 30 minutes   **Total time:** About 3 hours

1. For marinade and dressing, combine lime juice, barbecue rub, garlic, cumin and salt in **Small Batter Bowl**. Slowly add oil, whisking until well blended. For chicken, cut into thin strips and place in resealable plastic bag; add 1/4 cup (50 mL) marinade. Seal bag; turn to coat. Marinate in refrigerator 30-60 minutes. (Cover remaining marinade and refrigerate for use as dressing.)

2. Meanwhile, if desired, prepare *Barbecue Tortilla Chips* and set aside. Heat oil in **Grill Pan** over medium heat 5 minutes. Add corn, bell pepper and onion; spread evenly over bottom of pan. Cook without stirring 5 minutes or until grill marks appear on vegetables. Remove vegetable mixture to **Stainless (4-qt./4 L) Mixing Bowl**. Increase heat to medium-high. Remove chicken from marinade; discard marinade. Cook chicken 5-7 minutes or until no longer pink, turning occasionally. Remove from heat.

3. Add chicken, black beans and reserved dressing to vegetable mixture; toss to coat. Cover; refrigerate about 2 hours or until chilled. For each serving, arrange jicama on serving plate. Top with salad. Serve with *Barbecue Tortilla Chips*, if desired.

Yield: 4 servings

U.S. Nutrients per serving: Calories 360, Total Fat 15 g, Saturated Fat 1.5 g, Cholesterol 65 mg, Carbohydrate 28 g, Protein 31 g, Sodium 650 mg, Fiber 7 g
U.S. Diabetic exchanges per serving: 1 starch, 1 vegetable, 4 low-fat meat, 1/2 fat (1 carb)

chef's corner

Roasting the vegetables in the Grill Pan gives them a sweet and smoky flavor. Be certain not to stir the vegetables or they will not blacken in the pan.

For *Barbecue Tortilla Chips*, preheat oven to 400°F (200°C). Brush one side of 4 (6-in./15 cm) corn tortillas with 1/2 tsp (2 mL) vegetable oil. Sprinkle with 1 tsp (5 mL) Sweet & Smoky Barbecue Rub and 1/4 tsp (1 mL) coarse salt. Cut each tortilla into four wedges and arrange in a single layer on **Large Round Stone**. Bake 11-13 minutes or until edges are lightly browned and crisp. Remove from baking stone; cool completely.
Yield: 16 chips

Berry & Kiwi Salad with Sweet Balsamic Dressing

Berry & Kiwi Salad with Sweet Balsamic Dressing

The silky, pale green leaves of Boston lettuce pair beautifully with summer fruit and the subtle caramel flavor of the dressing.

Dressing

- 1/2 cup (125 mL) white balsamic vinegar
- 2 tbsp (30 mL) sugar
- 1/4 cup (50 mL) heavy whipping cream

Salad

- Almond Clusters (optional, see Chef's Corner)
- 1 small head Boston or bibb lettuce
- 1 cup (250 mL) strawberries, hulled and halved
- 1 cup (250 mL) blackberries or blueberries
- 2 kiwi, peeled and cut into wedges

Prep time: 15 minutes   **Total time:** About 1 hour

1. For dressing, whisk vinegar and sugar in **(1.5-qt./1.5 L) Saucepan** using **Silicone Sauce Whisk**. Bring to a boil; reduce heat to medium and cook 6-8 minutes or until mixture is reduced by half (1/4 cup/50 mL). Slowly whisk in cream; cook without stirring 2 minutes. Remove from heat; cool. Cover; refrigerate until ready to serve.

2. If desired, prepare *Almond Clusters* and set aside. For salad, discard any bruised outer leaves from head of lettuce. Gently wash lettuce and berries in separate colanders of **Salad and Berry Spinner**; spin dry. (Keep the small lettuce leaves whole and tear larger outer leaves, if necessary.) For each serving, place lettuce into serving bowl. Arrange strawberries, blackberries and kiwi over lettuce. Drizzle with about 1 tbsp (15 mL) dressing; serve with *Almond Clusters*, if desired. (Cover and refrigerate any remaining dressing for another use.)

Yield: 4 servings

LIGHT • U.S. Nutrients per serving (about 1 cup/250 mL salad and 1 tbsp/15 mL dressing): Calories 120, Total Fat 3.5 g, Saturated Fat 1.5 g, Cholesterol 10 mg, Carbohydrate 23 g, Protein 2 g, Sodium 5 mg, Fiber 3 g
U.S. Diabetic exchanges per serving (about 1 cup/250 mL salad and 1 tbsp/15 mL dressing): 1 1/2 fruit, 1/2 vegetable, 1/2 fat (1 1/2 carb)

chef's corner

The term "reduce" means to boil down to reduce the volume of a mixture. For the dressing, the vinegar and sugar mixture is boiled until it is reduced by about half the original amount. The whipping cream thickens the dressing, adding a silky texture and slight caramel flavor when heated further.

For *Almond Clusters*, combine 1/4 cup (50 mL) sliced almonds, 2 tsp (10 mL) corn syrup and 1/2 tsp (2 mL) sugar in **(8-in./20 cm) Sauté Pan**; toss to coat. Cook and stir over medium-high heat 5-7 minutes or until almonds begin to brown, stirring frequently. Immediately remove from pan onto **Parchment Paper**; cool completely. Break into clusters.

Bistro Steak Salad with Creamy Peppercorn Dressing

Bistro Steak Salad with Creamy Peppercorn Dressing

This tender steak salad strikes the perfect balance between substantial and elegant.

Dressing

- ¼ cup (50 mL) mayonnaise
- 2½ tsp (12 mL) milk
- 1½ tsp (7 mL) white wine vinegar
- 1 tsp (5 mL) Dijon mustard
- 1 tbsp (15 mL) snipped fresh chives
- 1 tsp (5 mL) **Crushed Peppercorn & Garlic Rub**

Salad and Steaks

- *Lacy Parmesan Baskets* (optional, see Chef's Corner)
- 4 cups (1 L) torn Boston or bibb lettuce
- ½ cup (125 mL) red grapes
- 1½ tsp (7 mL) Crushed Peppercorn & Garlic Rub
- 2 beef tenderloin steaks, cut 1½ in. (4 cm) thick (6-8 oz/175-250 g each)
- 1 tbsp (15 mL) snipped fresh chives

Prep time: 20 minutes **Total time:** About 45 minutes

1. For dressing, whisk ingredients using **Stainless Mini Whisk** in **Prep Bowl** until well blended. Cover; refrigerate until ready to use.

2. If desired, prepare *Lacy Parmesan Baskets* and set aside. For salad, gently wash lettuce and grapes in separate colanders of **Salad and Berry Spinner**; spin dry. Cut grapes in half; set grapes and lettuce aside. For steaks, rub peppercorn rub evenly over both sides of steaks. Heat **Grill Pan** over medium heat 5 minutes. Grill steaks 14-16 minutes or until **Pocket Thermometer** registers 155°F (68°C) for medium doneness, turning once. Remove steaks to **Cutting Board** and tent with aluminum foil; let stand 5 minutes or until internal temperature registers 160°F (71°C). Carve steaks into thin slices using **Chef's Knife**.

3. For each serving, arrange lettuce and grapes in Parmesan basket or on serving plate; top with steak slices. Drizzle with dressing; sprinkle with chives.

Yield: 2 servings

U.S. Nutrients per serving: Calories 530, Total Fat 37 g, Saturated Fat 9 g, Cholesterol 115 mg, Carbohydrate 12 g, Protein 37 g, Sodium 980 mg, Fiber 2 g
U.S. Diabetic exchanges per serving: 1 starch, 5 medium-fat meat, 2½ fat (1 carb)

chef's corner

For *Lacy Parmesan Baskets*, invert **Small Batter Bowl** over a 15-in. (38 cm) sheet of **Parchment Paper**. Grate 4 oz (125 g) fresh Parmesan cheese using **Deluxe Cheese Grater**. Heat **(10-in./25 cm) Skillet** over medium heat until hot. For each basket, sprinkle half of the cheese evenly over bottom of Skillet. When cheese begins to melt and surface turns light yellow, remove from heat and carefully invert Skillet above batter bowl. Starting at edge, gently peel cheese disk away from pan using **Classic Scraper**, allowing cheese to drape over bowl. Cool completely; remove from bowl. Repeat with remaining cheese. Yield: 2 baskets

Table for
2

Caramelized Pear and Blue Cheese Salad

Caramelized Pear and Blue Cheese Salad

For all its elegance, this is an easy salad to make. The reduced cranberry vinaigrette is a nice complement to the smooth sweetness of the pears.

Cranberry Vinaigrette

- 3/4 cup (175 mL) 100% cranberry juice
- 2 tbsp (30 mL) sugar
- 2 tsp (10 mL) red wine vinegar
- 1/2 tsp (2 mL) Dijon mustard
- 2 tsp (10 mL) vegetable oil

Salad

- 1 firm, ripe pear, such as Bartlett
- 1 tbsp (15 mL) butter
- 1 tbsp (15 mL) sugar
- 2 cups (500 mL) baby spring mix salad blend
- 2 tbsp (30 mL) coarsely chopped toasted walnuts
- 2 tbsp (30 mL) sweetened dried cranberries
- 1 oz (30 g) blue cheese, cut into thin slices

Prep time: 30 minutes   **Total time:** About 1 hour

1. For cranberry vinaigrette, whisk juice and sugar in **(8-in./20 cm) Sauté Pan** using **Silicone Sauce Whisk**. Bring to a boil; reduce heat to medium and cook 13-15 minutes or until mixture is reduced to 1/4 cup (50 mL). Remove from heat; cool slightly. Pour mixture into **Small Batter Bowl**; whisk in vinegar and mustard. Slowly add oil, whisking until well blended. Cover; refrigerate until ready to use.

2. For salad, cut pear in half lengthwise. Remove seeds from pear halves using **Core & More**. Melt butter in same Sauté Pan over medium-low heat. Whisk in sugar, spreading mixture evenly over bottom of pan. Place pear halves, cut side down, in pan. Cook 8-10 minutes or until pear halves are tender and cut surface is golden brown; remove from heat.

3. For each serving, arrange half of the salad blend on serving plate. Sprinkle with walnuts and cranberries. Top with pear half. Drizzle with vinaigrette. Garnish with cheese.

Yield: 2 servings

U.S. Nutrients per serving: Calories 390, Total Fat 20 g, Saturated Fat 7 g, Cholesterol 30 mg, Carbohydrate 52 g, Protein 6 g, Sodium 280 mg, Fiber 4 g
U.S. Diabetic exchanges per serving: 2 starch, 1 fruit, 4 fat (3 carb)

chef's corner

To caramelize means to cook the pears in sugar in order to turn them brown, giving them a sweet, caramel-like flavor. Green or red pears are equally suited for this salad.

Reducing the cranberry juice until a portion of it evaporates concentrates the flavor and color of the liquid for the vinaigrette. Adding a small amount of Dijon mustard to the vinaigrette will keep it from separating.

Table for

2

Fresh Beet Salad with Orange Vinaigrette

Fresh Beet Salad with Orange Vinaigrette

This colorful salad with crisp and tender textures is a perfect autumn side. Cooking the beets in orange juice infuses them with a fresh citrus flavor.

Beets

- 8 medium fresh beets, scrubbed
- 1 can (12 oz or 355 mL) frozen orange juice concentrate, thawed, divided
- 1 cup (250 mL) water
- 1 tsp (5 mL) orange zest

Dressing and Salad

- 1 tbsp (15 mL) white wine vinegar
- 1 tbsp (15 mL) snipped fresh basil leaves
- 1/4 tsp (1 mL) salt
- 1/8 tsp (0.5 mL) coarsely ground black pepper
- 1 tbsp (15 mL) vegetable oil
- 2 large oranges, cut into segments (see Chef's Corner)
- 2 sweet onion slices, separated into rings
- 1 cup lightly packed frisée or endive
- 4 tbsp (60 mL) crumbled feta cheese
- Coarsely ground black pepper

Prep time: 15 minutes **Total time:** About 1 hour

1. For beets, trim greens and root ends from beets and peel. (Save greens for a sauté or stir-fry, if desired.) Cut beets into 1-in. (2.5 cm) wedges. Place beets, 1¼ cups (300 mL) of the orange juice concentrate (reserve remaining concentrate for dressing), water and orange zest in **(3-qt./2.8 L) Saucepan**; bring to a boil. Cover; reduce heat and simmer 35-40 minutes or just until beets are tender when pierced with **Paring Knife**. Drain beets, discarding cooking liquid. Cool beets slightly, then cover and refrigerate until ready to use in salad.

2. Meanwhile, for dressing, combine remaining ¼ cup (55 mL) orange juice concentrate, vinegar, basil, salt and black pepper in **Small Batter Bowl**. Slowly add oil, whisking until well blended. Cover and refrigerate until ready to use.

3. For salad, for each serving, arrange onion rings on serving plate; top with beets, orange segments, frisée and cheese. Drizzle with dressing. Sprinkle with black pepper.

Yield: 4 servings

U.S. Nutrients per serving: Calories 220, Total Fat 6 g, Saturated Fat 1.5 g, Cholesterol 10 mg, Carbohydrate 40 g, Protein 5 g, Sodium 370 mg, Fiber 4 g
U.S. Diabetic exchanges per serving: 2 fruit, 2 vegetable, 1 fat (2 carb)

chef's corner

Frisée is a curly-leafed green that adds lift and texture to salads. Cut off the stem end of the frisée and discard the tough outer leaves.

To avoid staining your hands, wear plastic gloves while working with fresh beets.

To make orange segments, cut off a thin slice from the top and bottom of the orange; stand upright. Cutting from top to bottom, carefully trim away peel and white membrane. Cut down both sides of membrane. Remove segment; repeat with remaining segments.

Grilled Antipasto and Orzo Salad

Grilled Antipasto and Orzo Salad

The mild anise flavor of fresh fennel and the creaminess of fontina cheese add a special touch to this Italian-style salad.

Dressing

- 1/4 cup (50 mL) snipped fresh parsley
- 3 tablespoons lemon juice
- 2 tsp (10 mL) snipped fresh oregano leaves
- 2 tsp (10 mL) lemon zest
- 3/4 tsp (4 mL) salt
- 1 garlic clove, pressed
- 1/4 tsp (1 mL) coarsely ground black pepper
- 1/4 cup (50 mL) **Garlic Oil** or olive oil

Salad

- 8 oz (250 g) uncooked orzo pasta
- 1 small fennel bulb
- 1 tsp (5 mL) Garlic Oil
- 1 large red bell pepper, diced
- 1 can (14 oz or 398 mL) artichoke hearts in water, drained, cut in half and patted dry
- 1/2 cup (125 mL) pitted green olives, coarsely chopped
- 2 ounces fontina cheese, cubed
- **Bell Pepper Boats** (optional, see Chef's Corner)
- 1 package (3 oz/90 g) prosciutto (optional)

Prep time: 30 minutes   **Total time:** About 1 hour

1. For dressing, combine parsley, lemon juice, oregano, lemon zest, salt, garlic and black pepper in **Small Batter Bowl**. Slowly add oil, whisking until well blended. Cover; refrigerate until ready to use.

2. For salad, cook orzo according to package directions in **(2-qt./1.8 L) Saucepan**; drain and rinse under cold running water. Place orzo in **Stainless (4-qt./4 L) Mixing Bowl**. Slice fennel bulb crosswise into 1/4-in. (6 mm) slices; cut slices in half. Heat oil in **Grill Pan** over medium heat 5 minutes. Add fennel, bell pepper and artichokes. Cook without stirring 3 minutes. Stir and cook 2-3 minutes or until grill marks appear on vegetables. Remove vegetables to mixing bowl. Add olives, cheese and dressing; toss to coat. Serve at room temperature or cover and refrigerate until ready to serve.

3. Meanwhile, prepare *Bell Pepper Boats*, if desired. For each serving, place pepper half on serving plate; top with salad. Serve with slices of prosciutto, if desired.

Yield: 4 servings

U.S. Nutrients per serving: Calories 360, Total Fat 15 g, Saturated Fat 1.5 g, Cholesterol 65 mg, Carbohydrate 28 g, Protein 31 g, Sodium 650 mg, Fiber 7 g
U.S. Diabetic exchanges per serving: 3 starch, 1 vegetable, 1 medium-fat meat, 3 fat (3 carb)

chef's corner

Fresh fennel has a broad, bulbous base with celery-like stems and bright green foliage. It has a mild anise flavor. Wash the fennel, trim the base and slice bulb crosswise into 1/4-in. (6 mm) slices.

Fontina cheese is a semi-firm cow's milk cheese from Italy. It is pale yellow with a mild, nutty flavor.

For *Bell Pepper Boats*, cut two red bell peppers in half lengthwise; remove seeds and membranes. Heat Grill Pan over medium heat 5 minutes. Place bell peppers cut-side down on pan. Cook 2-4 minutes or until grill marks appear. Remove from pan; cool completely.
Yield: 4 boats

Grilled Asian Pork Tenderloin Salad

Grilled Asian Pork Tenderloin Salad

This exceptional salad features the complex flavor of our Asian Seasoning Mix. Grilling the pork in the Grill Pan is quick and flavorful.

Dressing

- 3 tbsp (45 mL) rice vinegar
- 1½ tbsp (22 mL) soy sauce
- 2 tsp (10 mL) **Asian Seasoning Mix**
- 1 tsp (5 mL) sugar
- ⅓ cup (75 mL) vegetable oil

Salad and Pork

- 5 cups (1.25 L) mixed salad greens
- 1 medium red bell pepper, cut into 2-in. (5 cm) strips
- 1 cup (250 mL) snow peas
- ½ red onion, sliced into thin wedges
- ⅓ cup (75 mL) snipped fresh cilantro
- 2 tbsp (30 mL) Asian Seasoning Mix
- 1 tbsp (15 mL) vegetable oil
- 1 pork tenderloin, about 1 lb (500 g)
- ¼ cup (50 mL) dry roasted peanuts, coarsely chopped (optional)

Prep time: 20 minutes   **Total time:** About 45 minutes

1. For dressing, combine vinegar, soy sauce, seasoning mix and sugar in **Small Batter Bowl**. Slowly add oil, whisking until well blended. Cover; refrigerate until ready to use.

2. For salad, arrange greens on large serving platter. Top with bell pepper, snow peas, onion and cilantro. Cover; refrigerate until ready to serve.

3. Heat **Grill Pan** over medium heat 5 minutes. For pork, combine seasoning mix and oil in **Prep Bowl**; rub over entire surface of pork. Grill pork 15-18 minutes or until **Pocket Thermometer** registers 155°F (68°C) for medium doneness or 165°F (75°C) for well done, turning every 5 minutes. Remove pork to **Cutting Board** and tent with aluminum foil; let stand 5-10 minutes.

4. To serve, carve pork into thin slices and arrange around edge of salad on serving platter. Sprinkle with peanuts, if desired. Drizzle with dressing.

Yield: 4 servings

U.S. Nutrients per serving: Calories 410, Total Fat 29 g, Saturated Fat 4 g, Cholesterol 75 mg, Carbohydrate 10 g, Protein 27 g, Sodium 460 mg, Fiber 4 g
U.S. Diabetic exchanges per serving: ½ fruit, 4 medium-fat meat, 2 fat (½ carb)

chef's corner

To ensure even cooking, be sure to turn the pork in the Grill Pan every 5 minutes using the **Chef's Tongs**. The internal temperature of the pork will rise approximately 5-10°F after it is removed from the pan.

For brighter color, blanch the snow peas in boiling water for 30 seconds, then drain and immediately plunge peas into a bowl of ice water to stop the cooking process. Let stand 5 minutes and drain. Pat dry with paper towels.

Grilled Georgia Peach and Chicken Salad

Grilled Georgia Peach and Chicken Salad

Watercress, with its tender and peppery leaves, mingles with sun-ripened peaches, chunks of grilled chicken and fresh mint for a lively summer salad.

Dressing

- 1/3 cup (75 mL) plain nonfat yogurt
- 1 tbsp (15 mL) fresh lime juice
- 1 tbsp (15 mL) peach preserves
- 1 tbsp (15 mL) snipped fresh mint leaves
- 1/8 tsp (0.5 mL) salt

Chicken and Salad

- 1 tsp (5 mL) vegetable oil
- 1 garlic clove, pressed
- 4 boneless, skinless chicken breast halves (4-6 oz/125-175 g each)
- Salt and coarsely ground black pepper
- *Grilled Cornbread Wedges* (optional, see Chef's Corner)

- 2 large peaches, pitted and cut into 3/4-in. (2 cm) wedges
- 1 cup (250 mL) lightly packed watercress leaves
- 1/4 cup (50 mL) toasted chopped pecans

Prep time: 30 minutes   **Total time:** About 2 hours, 30 minutes

1. For dressing, whisk ingredients in **Small Batter Bowl** until well blended. Cover; refrigerate until ready to use.

2. Prepare grill for direct cooking over medium coals. Meanwhile, for chicken, combine oil and garlic in **Prep Bowl**; brush over chicken. Season with salt and black pepper.

3. If desired, prepare *Grilled Cornbread Wedges* and set aside. For salad, place peach wedges on lightly greased grid of grill. Grill, covered, 2-3 minutes, carefully turning once using **Barbecue Turner** when grill marks appear. Remove peaches from grill. Place chicken on grid of grill. Grill, covered, 12-15 minutes or until chicken is no longer pink in center, turning occasionally. Remove chicken from grill; cut into 1/2-in. (1 cm) cubes. Place chicken and peaches in **Stainless (4-qt./4 L) Mixing Bowl**; add dressing and mix gently. Cover; refrigerate about 2 hours or until chilled.

4. To serve, add watercress to chicken mixture; toss lightly. Place on serving plates. Sprinkle with pecans. Serve with *Grilled Cornbread Wedges*, if desired.

Yield: 4 servings

U.S. Nutrients per serving: Calories 240, Total Fat 8 g, Saturated Fat 1 g, Cholesterol 65 mg, Carbohydrate 14 g, Protein 29 g, Sodium 230 mg, Fiber 2 g
U.S. Diabetic exchanges per serving: 1 fruit, 4 low-fat meat (1 carb)

chef's corner

Watercress has small, smooth leaves and is sold in bunches. Separate the watercress and break off the small branches from the thick main stems. Discard any leaves that are bruised or yellow. Gently wash the leaves using the **Salad and Berry Spinner** and spin dry.

For *Grilled Cornbread Wedges*, cut purchased cornbread into wedges; split in half horizontally. Place cornbread on lightly greased grid of grill. Grill, uncovered, 30-60 seconds or until grill marks appear.

Japanese-Style Wasabi Steak Salad

Japanese-Style Wasabi Steak Salad

This exotic salad, featuring a nice textural contrast between rice noodles and crisp vegetables, uses part of the wasabi salad dressing as a marinade for the steak.

Marinade and Dressing

- 6 tbsp (90 mL) rice vinegar
- 1 tbsp (15 mL) prepared wasabi paste
- 2 tsp (5 mL) **Asian Seasoning Mix**
- 1/2 tsp (2 mL) salt
- 1/4 tsp (1 mL) coarsely ground black pepper
- 1/2 cup (125 mL) dark sesame oil

Steak and Salad

- 1 flank steak (about 1-1 1/2 lb/500-750 g)
- 1/2 package (8 oz/250 g) uncooked straight-cut rice noodles
- 1 small carrot, peeled and cut into julienne strips
- 3 radishes, sliced
- 2 cups (500 mL) sugar snap peas
- 1/2 seedless cucumber, scored and sliced
- 1/4 cup (50 mL) toasted sesame seeds

Prep time: 30 minutes   **Total time:** About 3 hours, 30 minutes

1. For marinade and dressing, combine first five ingredients in **Small Batter Bowl**. Slowly add oil, whisking until well blended. For steak, place flank steak in resealable plastic bag; add 1/4 cup (50 mL) of the marinade. Seal bag; turn to coat. Marinate in refrigerator 3 hours or overnight. (Cover remaining marinade and refrigerate for use as dressing.)

2. Meanwhile, for salad, cook noodles according to package directions in **(4-qt./4 L) Casserole**. Drain and rinse under cold water; place in **Stainless (4-qt./4 L) Mixing Bowl**. Add carrot, radishes and peas to noodles. Reserve 2 tbsp (30 mL) of the dressing. Pour remaining dressing over noodle mixture; toss to coat. Cover; refrigerate until ready to serve.

3. Heat **Grill Pan** over medium heat 5 minutes. Remove steak from marinade; discard marinade. Grill steak 15-20 minutes or until **Pocket Thermometer** registers 140°F (63°C) for medium-rare doneness or 155°F (68°C) for medium doneness, turning occasionally. Remove steak to cutting board; let stand 5 minutes. Carve steak diagonally across the grain into thin slices.

4. For each serving, arrange noodle mixture, cucumber slices and steak on serving plate. Drizzle 2 tbsp (30 mL) reserved dressing over salad. Sprinkle with sesame seeds.

Yield: 4-6 servings

U.S. Nutrients per serving: Calories 700, Total Fat 32 g, Saturated Fat 7 g, Cholesterol 40 mg, Carbohydrate 57 g, Protein 29 g, Sodium 520 mg, Fiber 4 g
U.S. Diabetic exchanges per serving: 3 starch, 1 fruit, 4 medium-fat meat, 2 fat (4 carb)

chef's corner

Flank steak is a flat cut of beef that is best when marinated in order to tenderize it. Once cooked, it must be carved across the grain so that the slices are tender, rather than stringy and fibrous. To cut diagonally across the grain, check for the direction the meat fibers are running, then cut crosswise into thin slices, angling the knife slightly.

The temperature of the steak will rise approximately 5°F after it is removed from the pan.

Wasabi, which comes from the root of an Asian plant, is the Japanese version of horseradish and is served with sushi and other dishes as a condiment. It is light green and has a sharp, fiery flavor.

Jerk Shrimp, Mango & Avocado Salad

Jerk Shrimp, Mango & Avocado Salad

"Jerk" refers to an authentic Jamaican way to cook meat, poultry and seafood. But it's the combination of spicy and sweet seasonings that makes jerk what it is.

Dressing

- 2 tbsp (30 mL) lime juice
- 1 tbsp (15 mL) sugar
- 1 tsp (5 mL) lime zest
  Dash of salt
- 2 tbsp (30 mL) vegetable oil

Shrimp and Salad

- 1 tbsp (15 mL) lime juice
- 1 tbsp (15 mL) **Jamaican Jerk Rub**
- 2 tsp (10 mL) vegetable oil
- 2 tsp (10 mL) finely chopped jalapeño pepper
- 1 garlic clove, pressed
- 16 large uncooked shrimp (21-25 per pound), peeled and deveined, tails removed

- 1 firm, ripe avocado
- 1 head Belgian endive, separated into leaves
- 1 firm, ripe mango, peeled and cut into cubes
- 1/4 cup (50 mL) chopped red bell pepper
  Lime wedges

Prep time: 15 minutes **Total time:** About 30 minutes

1. For dressing, combine lime juice, sugar, lime zest and salt in **Small Batter Bowl**. Slowly add oil, whisking until well blended. Cover; refrigerate until ready to serve.

2. For shrimp, in **Classic Batter Bowl**, whisk lime juice, jerk rub, oil, jalapeño pepper and garlic until well blended. Add shrimp and toss to coat. Cover; refrigerate 15 minutes.

3. Heat **(10-in./25 cm) Skillet** over medium heat until a drop of water sizzles. Add shrimp and cook 4-6 minutes or until shrimp turns opaque and is cooked through, turning once. Remove from Skillet.

4. For salad, peel and slice avocado using **Utility Knife**. For each serving, arrange avocado slices and endive leaves on serving plate. Top with mango and bell pepper; drizzle with dressing. Arrange shrimp next to salad. Serve with lime wedges.

Yield: 2 servings

U.S. Nutrients per serving: Calories 360, Total Fat 15 g, Saturated Fat 1.5 g, Cholesterol 65 mg, Carbohydrate 28 g, Protein 31 g, Sodium 650 mg, Fiber 7 g
U.S. Diabetic exchanges per serving: 2 fruit, 2 low-fat meat, 6 fat (2 carb)

chef's corner

To peel a mango, use the **Santoku Knife** to cut off top and bottom of fruit. Stand fruit upright, stem end down, on **Cutting Board**. Carefully cut off peel from top to bottom. Rub the top of the mango with your thumb to determine the direction of the large, flat pit. Slice off flesh alongside the pit. Cut flesh into cubes.

Belgian endive is a small cigar-shaped head of white, tightly packed leaves with yellow tips. It becomes bitter when exposed to light, so it is best wrapped in a damp paper towel, then placed in a resealable plastic bag and refrigerated for no longer than a day.

King Crab Salad with Lemon Crêpes

King Crab Salad with Lemon Crêpes

The extra effort of shelling king crab legs and preparing the accompanying crêpes is worthwhile: this salad is truly special and guaranteed to impress.

Salad and Dressing

- 8 oz (250 g) cooked king crabmeat (about 1 lb/500 g crab legs in shells)
- ¹/₂ cup (125 mL) canned hearts of palm, drained and sliced
- ¹/₂ cup (125 mL) sliced celery
- ¹/₂ cup (125 mL) chopped red onion
- 1 lemon
- 2 tbsp (30 mL) mayonnaise
- 1 tsp (5 mL) hot pepper sauce
- 1 garlic clove, pressed
- 1 tsp (5 mL) snipped fresh dill weed

Cucumber ribbons (optional, see Chef's Corner)

Fresh dill sprigs (optional)

Crêpes

- ¹/₃ cup (75 mL) milk
- 1 egg
- 3 tbsp (45 mL) all-purpose flour
- 3 tsp (15 mL) melted butter
- 2 tsp (10 mL) sugar
- ¹/₄ tsp (1 mL) salt

chef's corner

To remove crabmeat from shell, carefully cut down length of shell using **Kitchen Shears**. Split shell apart to remove meat. Place the meat on paper towels to absorb any excess moisture.

Crêpes can be made ahead of time and stacked between squares of **Parchment Paper**. Place in resealable plastic bag and refrigerate or freeze until ready to use. Microwave for a few seconds or until warm before serving.

To make cucumber ribbons, cut ends from half of an English (seedless) cucumber. Using **Vegetable Peeler**, slice down length of cucumber to make thin ribbons.

Prep time: 30 minutes   **Total time:** About 1 hour

1. For salad, remove crabmeat from shells and place in **Classic Batter Bowl** (see Chef's Corner). Add hearts of palm, celery and onion. For dressing, zest lemon using **Microplane® Adjustable Grater** to measure 2 tsp (10 mL) zest. Juice lemon to measure 1 tbsp (15 mL) juice. In **Small Batter Bowl**, whisk mayonnaise, half of the zest (set aside remaining zest for crêpes), juice, hot pepper sauce, garlic and dill weed until well blended. Add dressing to crabmeat mixture; mix gently. Cover and refrigerate until ready to serve.

2. For crêpes, whisk together milk, egg, flour, butter, sugar, salt and reserved lemon zest in **Stainless (2-qt./2 L) Mixing Bowl** until smooth. Heat **(8-in./20 cm) Sauté Pan** over medium heat until a drop of water sizzles, then evaporates; grease lightly. Pour scant ¹/₄ cup (50 mL) batter into pan, immediately tilting and swirling pan to cover bottom. When crêpe starts to bubble and edges are brown, turn using **Small Slotted Turner**. Cook about 1 additional minute or until lightly browned. Remove from pan. Repeat with remaining batter.

3. To serve, spoon salad over cucumber ribbons; garnish with fresh dill sprigs, if desired. Serve with crêpes.

Yield: 2 servings

U.S. Nutrients per serving (1 cup/250 mL salad, 2 crêpes): Calories 410, Total Fat 22 g, Saturated Fat 7 g, Cholesterol 190 mg, Carbohydrate 23 g, Protein 29 g, Sodium 1870 mg, Fiber 3 g
U.S. Diabetic exchanges per serving (1 cup/250 mL salad, 2 crêpes): 1¹/₂ starch, 3¹/₂ low-fat meat, 2 fat (1¹/₂ carb)

Table for

2

Potato and Green Bean Salad with Fresh Pesto

Potato and Green Bean Salad with Fresh Pesto

Fresh basil pesto adds exhilarating flavor to so many summer dishes including this combination of roasted potatoes, fresh green beans and red onion.

Salad

- 1¹/₂ lb (750 g) fingerling potatoes, quartered lengthwise
- 1 tbsp (15 mL) **Basil Oil** or olive oil
- ³/₄ tsp (4 mL) salt
- ¹/₂ lb (250 g) fresh green beans
- ¹/₂ small red onion

Basil Pesto

- ¹/₂ cup (125 mL) lightly packed fresh basil leaves
- ¹/₄ cup (50 mL) toasted pine nuts
- 2 tbsp (30 mL) Basil Oil
- 1 tbsp (15 mL) white balsamic vinegar
- 1 garlic clove, pressed
- ¹/₈ tsp (0.5 mL) coarsely ground black pepper

Prep time: 15 minutes   **Total time:** About 45 minutes

1. Preheat oven to 450°F (230°C). For salad, toss potatoes, oil and salt in **Stainless (4-qt./4 L) Mixing Bowl**. Arrange potatoes in a single layer on **Large Bar Pan**. Bake 20-25 minutes or until tender, stirring halfway through baking; remove from oven.

2. Meanwhile, cut green beans in half; blanch and set aside (see Chef's Corner). Slice onion into thin wedges using **Chef's Knife**. For basil pesto, place basil and pine nuts on **Cutting Board**; finely chop together using **Food Chopper**. Place basil mixture in **Small Batter Bowl**; add oil, vinegar, garlic and black pepper and whisk until well blended.

3. Combine potatoes, green beans and onion in same Stainless (4-qt./4 L) Mixing Bowl. Pour basil mixture over vegetables, tossing to coat. Serve at room temperature.

Yield: 6 servings

U.S. Nutrients per serving (1 cup/250 mL): Calories 130, Total Fat 11 g, Saturated Fat 1 g, Cholesterol 0 mg, Carbohydrate 9 g, Protein 2 g, Sodium 290 mg, Fiber 2 g
U.S. Diabetic exchanges per serving (1 cup/250 mL): ¹/₂ starch, 2 fat (¹/₂ carb)

chef's corner

To blanch means to boil in water for a short time. It is done for a variety of purposes: as a preliminary cooking process; as a way of setting color; or as a way of easily removing peels from vegetables or fruits.

To blanch green beans, bring salted water to a boil in **(2-qt./1.8 L) Saucepan**. Add green beans; cook 3-4 minute or until crisp-tender. Drain using **Strainer** and immediately plunge into a bowl of ice water to stop the cooking process. Let stand 5 minutes and drain. Pat dry with paper towels.

Petite golden or red potatoes, halved, can be substituted for the fingerling potatoes, if desired.

Quinoa Salad with Shiitake Mushrooms and Leeks

Quinoa Salad with Shiitake Mushrooms and Leeks

The earthy flavors of quinoa (pronounced KEEN-wah), mushrooms and goat cheese are wonderfully balanced by the classic vinaigrette dressing in this easy-to-make side dish.

Dressing

- 2 tbsp (30 mL) red wine vinegar
- 1 garlic clove, pressed
- 1/4 tsp (1 mL) salt
- 1 tbsp (15 mL) olive oil

Salad

- 3/4 cup (175 mL) quinoa (see Chef's Corner)
- 1 1/2 cups (375 mL) water
- 5 dried shiitake mushrooms, sliced
- 1/2 tsp (2 mL) salt
- 2 leeks, white and light green portions only
- 1 tbsp (15 mL) snipped fresh mint leaves
- 2 oz (60 g) goat cheese, crumbled

Prep time: 20 minutes   **Total time:** About 30 minutes

1. For dressing, whisk vinegar, garlic pressed with **Garlic Press** and salt in **Small Batter Bowl**. Slowly add oil, whisking until well blended, set aside.

2. For salad, place quinoa, water, shiitake mushrooms and salt in **(3-qt./2.8 L) Saucepan**; bring to a boil. Cover; reduce heat to low and simmer 15 minutes. Remove from heat and set aside.

3. Meanwhile, cut leeks in half lengthwise, then into 4-in. (10 cm) pieces using **Santoku Knife**. Heat **Grill Pan** over medium-high heat 5 minutes. Place leeks in pan; brush with some of the dressing using **Chef's Silicone Basting Brush**. Place **Grill Press** over leeks; grill 3-5 minutes, turning once. Remove leeks from pan; cool slightly, then cut into thin slices.

4. Snip mint using **Kitchen Shears**. In **Stainless (2-qt./2 L) Mixing Bowl**, combine quinoa mixture, leeks, mint, goat cheese and remaining dressing; mix gently. Serve warm or at room temperature.

Yield: 4 servings

U.S. Nutrients per serving (about 1/2 cup/125 mL): Calories 240, Total Fat 10 g, Saturated Fat 3.5 g, Cholesterol 10 mg, Carbohydrate 32 g, Protein 8 g, Sodium 530 mg, Fiber 3 g
U.S. Diabetic exchanges per serving (about 1/2 cup/125 mL): 2 starch, 1/2 vegetable, 2 fat (2 carb)

chef's corner

Quinoa is an ivory, bead-shaped seed that is treated like a grain and has a delicate flavor. It is considered a "super grain" because it contains all eight essential amino acids.

Couscous can be substituted for the quinoa, if desired. Add the shiitake mushrooms and salt to the water and bring to a boil. Add the couscous. Remove from heat and cover to hydrate.

Dry shiitake mushrooms need to be hydrated before using and have a concentrated flavo and meaty texture.

Cut leeks in half lengthwise before washing to remove any grit. The white and light green parts of the leek are the most tender portions; do not use the dark green leaves.

Roasted Sweet Potato Salad with Citrus-Curry Dressing

Roasted Sweet Potato Salad with Citrus-Curry Dressing

The peppery bite of arugula leaves pairs deliciously with tender sweet potatoes, crisp apple chunks and the distinctive curry dressing.

Salad

- *Spiced Walnuts* (optional, see Chef's Corner)
- 3 large sweet potatoes, peeled (about 2 lb/1 kg)
- 1 tbsp (15 mL) olive oil
- Salt and coarsely ground black pepper
- 1 medium Red Delicious apple, cored and diced
- 1/2 cup (125 mL) diced celery
- 1/4 cup (50 mL) thinly sliced green onions with tops
- 1 package (5 oz/150 g) fresh arugula

Dressing

- 1/4 cup (50 mL) light mayonnaise
- 1/4 cup (50 mL) fresh orange juice
- 1 tbsp (15 mL) prepared stone-ground Dijon mustard
- 1 tsp (5 mL) curry powder
- 1 tsp (5 mL) orange zest

Prep time: 25 minutes **Total time:** About 50 minutes

1. If desired, prepare *Spiced Walnuts* and set aside. For salad, preheat oven to 450°F (230°C). Cut potatoes crosswise into 1/2-in. (1 cm) slices; cut slices into quarters. Brush **Large Bar Pan** with oil using **Chef's Silicone Basting Brush**. Arrange potatoes in a single layer on bar pan; season with salt and black pepper. Bake 22-24 minutes or until potatoes are tender and begin to caramelize, stirring halfway through baking. Remove from oven; cool slightly. Place potatoes in **Stainless (4-qt./4 L) Mixing Bowl**. Add apple, celery and green onions. Gently wash arugula in **Salad and Berry Spinner**; spin dry.

2. For dressing, whisk ingredients in **Small Batter Bowl** until well blended. Drizzle 1/3 cup (75 mL) of the dressing over potato mixture; toss gently to coat.

3. For each serving, place arugula on serving plate; drizzle with some of the remaining dressing. Mound potato mixture over arugula. Sprinkle with *Spiced Walnuts*, if desired.

Yield: 6 servings

U.S. Nutrients per serving (about 1 1/2 cups/375 mL): Calories 190, Total Fat 6 g, Saturated Fat 1 g, Cholesterol 5 mg, Carbohydrate 32 g, Protein 4 g, Sodium 250 mg, Fiber 6 g
U.S. Diabetic exchanges per serving (about 1 1/2 cups/375 mL): 1 starch, 1 fruit, 1 fat (1 carb)

chef's corner

To make *Spiced Walnuts*, preheat oven to 350°F (180°C). Line **Small Bar Pan** with **Parchment Paper**. Whisk 1 egg white in Small Batter Bowl until frothy. Add 1/2 cup (125 mL) walnut halves, tossing to coat. Arrange walnuts in a single layer over parchment. Combine 2 tbsp (30 mL) brown sugar and 1/4 tsp (1 mL) **Cinnamon Plus® Spice Blend** or **Korintje Cinnamon**; sprinkle over walnuts. Bake 18-20 minutes or until nuts begin to brown. Remove from oven. Cool completely.

Roasted Vegetable Ribbon Salad

Roasted Vegetable Ribbon Salad

A lasagna noodle is intertwined with fresh greens and roasted vegetables for an interesting take on the basic marinated pasta salad.

Salad Mixture

- ½ yellow squash
- ½ zucchini
- 8 oz (250 g) fresh asparagus spears, cut into ½-in. (1 cm) lengths
- 1 cup (250 mL) grape tomatoes, cut in half
- 1 tsp (5 mL) **Basil Oil** or olive oil
- ¼ tsp (1 mL) **Citrus & Basil Rub**
- 1 garlic clove, pressed
- 1½ cups (375 mL) baby spring mix salad blend
- 1 oz (30 g) shaved fresh Parmesan cheese

Dressing

- 1 tbsp (15 mL) fresh lemon juice
- ¾ tsp (4 mL) Thai red curry paste
- ½ tsp (2 mL) Citrus & Basil Rub
- 2 tbsp (30 mL) Basil Oil

- 2 cooked lasagna noodles, chilled
- Additional shaved fresh Parmesan cheese for garnish (optional)

Prep time: 20 minutes   **Total time:** About 30 minutes

1. Preheat oven to 425°F (220°C). For salad mixture, slice yellow squash and zucchini lengthwise with **Ultimate Mandoline** fitted with v-shaped blade. Combine squash, zucchini, asparagus, tomatoes, oil, citrus rub and garlic in **Stainless (2-qt./2 L) Mixing Bowl**; toss to coat. Spread in a single layer on **Large Bar Pan**. Bake 10-12 minutes or until vegetables are tender; remove from oven and cool completely. Wash greens in **Salad and Berry Spinner**; spin dry.

2. For dressing, combine lemon juice, curry paste and citrus rub in **Small Batter Bowl**. Slowly add oil, whisking until well blended. Reserve 2 tsp (10 mL) of the dressing for serving. Place roasted vegetables, greens, cheese and remaining dressing in **Stainless (4-qt./4 L) Mixing Bowl**; toss to coat.

3. To assemble each salad, place end of one noodle on serving plate (a third of it should be on the center of the plate with two-thirds overhanging one side); top with ½ cup (125 mL) of the salad mixture. Fold over middle third of the lasagna noodle; top with additional ½ cup (125 mL) of the salad mixture. Fold back the final third of noodle, forming a vertical "s" shape. Top with small amount of salad mixture. Drizzle with 1 tsp (5 mL) of the reserved dressing. Garnish with additional shaved Parmesan cheese, if desired.

Yield: 2 servings

U.S. Nutrients per serving: Calories 360, Total Fat 22 g, Saturated Fat 4 g, Cholesterol 10 mg, Carbohydrate 31 g, Protein 14 g, Sodium 400 mg, Fiber 6 g
U.S. Diabetic exchanges per serving: 2 starch, 1 medium-fat meat, 3 fat (2 carb)

chef's corner

To keep the layers even, make sure there is a balanced amount of salad mixture on the noodle before placing the next layer on top. Mound the salad mixture as you layer to give the salad height.

Thai red curry paste is a blend of chilies, garlic, lemongrass and other seasonings. It can be found in the Asian section of larger supermarkets.

The **Vegetable Peeler** is a great tool to make shaved Parmesan cheese.

Table for

2

Tomato, Basil and Portobello Napoleons

Tomato, Basil and Portobello Napoleons

A spin-off of the layered French puff pastry dessert, these stacked salads are crowned with crispy breaded goat cheese rounds.

Dressing

- 2 tbsp (30 mL) white wine vinegar
- 1 garlic clove, pressed
- 1/4 tsp (1 mL) **Italian Seasoning Mix**
- 1/4 tsp (1 mL) salt
- 1 tbsp (15 mL) **Basil Oil** or olive oil

Napoleons

- 2 large tomatoes
- 1 pkg. (6 oz or 170 g) small portobello mushroom caps (about 6 mushrooms)
- 1 log (3.5-4 oz/100-125 g) goat cheese
- 1/3 cup (75 mL) pine nuts, grated
- 1/4 cup (50 mL) fresh bread crumbs
- 1/2 tsp (2 mL) Italian Seasoning Mix
- 1 tbsp (15 mL) Basil Oil
- 4 large basil leaves, thinly sliced
- Additional Basil Oil (optional)

Prep time: 35 minutes **Total time:** About 1 hour

1. Preheat oven to 450°F (230°C). For dressing, combine vinegar, garlic, seasoning mix and salt in **Small Batter Bowl**. Slowly add oil, whisking until well blended. For napoleons, cut each tomato into four 1/2-inch-thick (1 cm) slices. Place tomato slices and mushrooms on **Large Bar Pan** lined with **Parchment Paper**. Brush dressing on both sides of vegetables using **Chef's Silicone Basting Brush**. Bake 20-25 minutes, turning once. Remove from oven; cut mushrooms into 1/2-in. (1 cm) slices using **Utility Knife**.

2. Slice goat cheese evenly into eight rounds; form each slice into a ball. Combine nuts, bread crumbs and seasoning mix in shallow dish. Place each cheese ball into nut mixture. Press gently to flatten; turn to coat both sides. Heat oil in **(10-in./25 cm) Sauté Pan** over medium heat until hot. Cook goat cheese rounds 30-45 seconds on each side or until coating is light golden brown, turning with **Small Slotted Turner**. Remove from pan.

3. To assemble each napoleon, layer tomato slice, mushroom slices and basil; repeat layers one time. Top with two goat cheese rounds. Drizzle with additional oil, if desired.

Yield: 4 servings

U.S. Nutrients per serving: Calories 260, Total Fat 23 g, Saturated Fat 6 g, Cholesterol 20 mg, Carbohydrate 10 g, Protein 9 g, Sodium 300 mg, Fiber 2 g
U.S. Diabetic exchanges per serving: 2 vegetable, 1 high-fat meat, 3 fat (0 carb)

chef's corner

Goat cheese by nature is rather crumbly and tacky. Coatings tend to fall off easily if the cheese is simply sliced into rounds. Forming goat cheese slices into balls and pressing them into the pine nut mixture softens the cheese enough to let the coating adhere.

To thinly slice basil, stack the leaves and roll them into a tight cylinder. Using the **Chef's Knife**, slice the roll crosswise into thin strips. This technique is called chiffonade (shif-un-NAHD).

Tuscan Salmon and Bean Salad

This is a delicious example of a composed salad, in which ingredients are arranged rather than tossed together. In this case, each guest can build his or her own masterpiece.

Dressing

- 2 tbsp (30 mL) small capers, finely chopped
- 2 tbsp (30 mL) **Basil Oil** or olive oil
- 2 tbsp (30 mL) mayonnaise
- 1 tbsp (15 mL) red wine vinegar
- 1 tbsp (15 mL) snipped fresh basil
- 3 garlic cloves, pressed
- 1/2 shallot, finely chopped
- 1/2 tsp (2 mL) Dijon mustard
- 1/4 tsp (1 mL) salt
- 1/8 tsp (0.5 mL) coarsely ground black pepper

Bean Spread and Salad

- 1 can (15 oz or 540 mL) cannellini or white kidney beans, rinsed and drained, divided
- 1/4 cup (50 mL) finely chopped roasted red pepper
- 8 oz (250 g) skinless salmon fillet, poached (see Chef's Corner)
- 4 plum tomatoes, thinly sliced
- 1 tbsp (15 mL) small capers
- 8 thin slices ciabatta bread, toasted

chef's corner

For *Poached Salmon*, combine 1/2 cup (125 mL) dry white wine and 1/2 cup (125 mL) water in **(10-in./25 cm) Skillet**. Add 4 lemon slices, 4 sprigs fresh parsley and 4 whole black peppercorns; bring to a boil. Place salmon on top of lemon slices; cover. Reduce heat to a simmer; cook 7-9 minutes or until salmon flakes easily with a fork. Remove salmon from Skillet; cool completely. Flake into small chunks using a fork.

Prep time: 20 minutes **Total time:** About 2 hours, 30 minutes

1. For dressing, whisk ingredients in **Small Batter Bowl** until well blended. For bean spread, mash 1/2 cup (125 mL) of the beans with 1 tbsp (15 mL) of the dressing in **Prep Bowl**; cover and refrigerate until ready to use.

2. For salad, combine remaining beans, red pepper and poached salmon in **Stainless (2-qt./2 L) Mixing Bowl**. Drizzle 3/4 cup (175 mL) of the dressing over salad; toss gently to coat. Cover; refrigerate about 2 hours or until chilled.

3. When ready to serve, spoon bean spread evenly into small serving bowls. Arrange tomato and bread slices on serving plates; spoon salad next to tomatoes. Garnish with capers. To serve, spread bean spread on ciabatta bread slices; top with tomato slices and salad.

Yield: 4 servings

U.S. Nutrients per serving: Calories 440, Total Fat 21 g, Saturated Fat 3 g, Cholesterol 30 mg, Carbohydrate 44 g, Protein 19 g, Sodium 940 mg, Fiber 5 g
U.S. Diabetic exchanges per serving: 2½ starch, 2 medium-fat meat, 2 fat (2½ carb)

Wilted Spinach Salad with Candied Pepper Bacon

Wilted Spinach Salad with Candied Pepper Bacon

Sweet, peppery bacon stars in this updated version of a classic salad featuring tender spinach leaves gently softened by the warm, tangy vinaigrette.

Bacon and Salad

- 4 slices thick-cut bacon
- 1 tbsp (15 mL) packed brown sugar, divided
- 1/2 tsp (2 mL) coarsely ground black pepper
- 1 package (6 oz/175 g) fresh baby spinach
- 1 medium Granny Smith apple, cored and sliced into thin wedges
- 1/4 cup (50 mL) thinly sliced red onion wedges

Salt and coarsely ground black pepper
- 2 hard-cooked eggs, peeled and cut into wedges

Dressing

- 1 tbsp (15 mL) reserved drippings from bacon
- 2 tbsp (30 mL) brown sugar
- 1 1/2 tbsp (22 mL) apple cider vinegar
- 2 tsp (10 mL) Dijon mustard

Prep time: 15 minutes   **Total time:** About 30 minutes

1. For bacon, line **Small Bar Pan** with **Parchment Paper**. Arrange bacon slices in a single layer on bar pan; sprinkle evenly with brown sugar and black pepper. Microwave on HIGH 3-5 minutes or until crisp; drain on paper towels. Reserve 1 tbsp (15 mL) of the bacon drippings from bar pan. Cut bacon into 1/2-in. (1 cm) pieces using **Santoku Knife**; set aside.

2. For salad, wash spinach in **Salad and Berry Spinner**; spin dry. In **Stainless (4-qt./4 L) Mixing Bowl**, combine spinach, apple and onion. For dressing, whisk reserved 1 tbsp (15 mL) bacon drippings, brown sugar, vinegar and mustard in **Small Micro-Cooker®** until well blended. Cover; microwave on HIGH 2 minutes or until bubbly. To serve, pour dressing over spinach mixture; toss gently to coat. Season with salt and black pepper. Top salad with egg wedges and bacon pieces. Serve immediately.

Yield: 4 servings

U.S. Nutrients per serving: Calories 190, Total Fat 10 g, Saturated Fat 4 g, Cholesterol 120 mg, Carbohydrate 17 g, Protein 7 g, Sodium 460 mg, Fiber 2 g
U.S. Diabetic exchanges per serving: 1 fruit, 1 medium-fat meat, 1 fat (1 carb)

chef's corner

Thick-cut bacon is a good choice for this salad because it is sturdy and will crumble less after being cooked in the microwave oven. To prevent spattering, place another piece of parchment over the pan while microwaving the bacon.

Instead of using only spinach, try adding other greens such as frisée, escarole or endive to the spinach. Their slightly pungent flavor and crisp texture stand up well to this type of preparation.